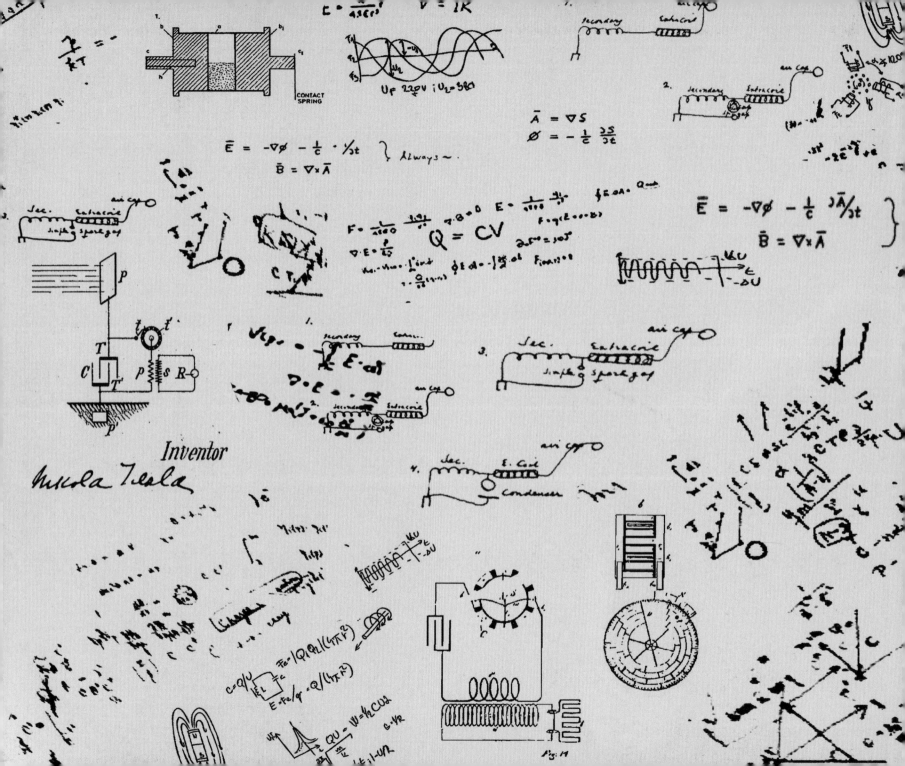

BRIGHT DREAMS

THE BRILLIANT IDEAS OF NIKOLA TESLA

by Tracy Dockray

CAPSTONE EDITIONS
a capstone imprint

NIKOLA TESLA, OF NEW YORK, N. Y.
ALTERNATING-ELECTRIC-CURRENT GENERATOR
No. 447,921. Patented Mar. 10, 189

N. TESLA.
ALTERNATING MOTOR.
No. 555,190. Patented Feb. 25, 1896.

Bright Dreams is published by Capstone Editions, an imprint of Capstone.
1710 Roe Crest Drive
North Mankato, Minnesota 56003
www.capstonepub.com

Library of Congress Cataloging-in-Publication Data is available on the Library of Congress website.
ISBN: 978-1-68446-141-7 (hardcover)
ISBN: 978-1-68446-142-4 (eBook PDF)

Summary: Young Nikola Tesla got a shock when he rubbed his cat's fur. That small spark lit his imagination forever. Covering his early years to his eventual success in the world of electricity, *Bright Dreams* showcases Tesla's incredible journey of discovery and perseverance. Author-illustrator Tracy Dockray conveys Tesla's busy and imaginative world with collage-style artwork and informative sidebars.

Image Credits
Albert Einstein: endsheet design; Dover Publications: Alexis Kravtchenko, 5, Archive from 19th Century Sources, 5, 18, Dover Publications, 8, Gustave Dore, 7, 11, 17, M. Dobuzinki, 9, S. Rice, 15, Victorian Fashion and Costumes, 15; Electrical World Magazine: W.J. Johnson Co.; Galileo: endsheet design; Isaac Newton: endsheet design; Library of Congress: Keppler Udo J, 20, 21; Edward J. Covington, 21; Michael Benabib, 30; Nikola Tesla: endsheet design; Picturesque World's Fair: W.B. Conkey, 24; Scientific American, 19; Srinavasa Ramanujan: endsheet design; Wikimedia: A.B. Frost, 16, American Fine Art Co, 25, A.P. Snyder Ha, Charles Graham, 21, Dörre Tivadar, 13, IEE Global History Network, 18, Internet Archive Book Images, 23, 25, Jacques Reich, 18, Joseph Gaylord Gessford, 23, L. Gaumont & Co., 20, Napoleon Sarong, 22, NASA/JPL/Cornell University, Maas Digital LLC, Nikola Tesla, cover, 26, Peter Salcher, 26, Professor Alexandra von Meier, cover, Steve Jurvetson, 26, The True Wireless, cover, Wellcome Image Gallery, 14, 20, William Maver, 20, W. P. Snyder, 22

Designed by Tracy Dockray and Ted Williams

All internet sites appearing in back matter were available and accurate when this book was sent to press.

Printed and bound in China. 3322

To Mr. Diveki and science teachers dedicated to
illuminating our understanding of the world around us.

Putovnica. Reisepass.

"Let the future tell the truth . . .
The present is theirs; the future, for which
I have really worked, is mine."

—Nikola Tesla, from "A Visit to Nikola
Tesla," by Dragislav L. Petkovic in *Politika*

Young Nikola got a shock when he rubbed his cat's fur. That small spark lit his imagination forever.

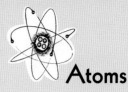 # Atoms

Atoms are the basic unit that make up all matter. Electrons are found in atoms. They are very small particles that have a negative charge of electricity. When objects are rubbed together, electrons can move from one object to another. If a cat rubs against a blanket, electrons can move from the blanket to the cat's fur. This could cause static electricity, or an imbalance of electrons on the cat's fur. When you touch the cat, those extra electrons seek balance. They shoot away from the cat through an electric charge. This can cause static shock.

Lightning happens in the sky when there is an excess electrical charge in or around the clouds. When the positive and negative charges grow large enough, a spark occurs between clouds or the clouds and Earth. This is like that spark on the cat's fur, only much, much **bigger**.

The night Nikola Tesla was born, bright electricity flashed above his family's home. Inside it was dim and quiet. No electric light brightened the room, nor did a radio, phone, television, or computer break the silence. It was 1856, and none had been invented . . . yet.

Nikola's father was a respected priest in the nearby church, but it was his mother who young Nikola most admired. She invented clever tools for their home. She entertained her children by reciting tales of brave knights and kings. Nikola was surrounded by invention and imagination.

Nikola's Early Experiments

Bug-Powered Propeller

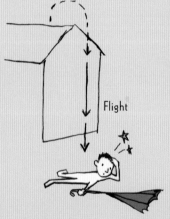

Flight

Water Power

Nikola had three busy sisters and a big brother. Everyone admired the older boy's intelligence and daring personality. Nikola, on the other hand, was always distracted and dreaming.

He dreamed about his inventions all the time. It was while Nikola was working on his first small creation that he saw his brother fall.

The family was heartbroken
by the fatal accident. Nikola had
always admired his brother. Could
he ever be strong and bold like him?

Nikola wasn't mighty, but he was imaginative, smart, and loved to learn. Nothing could stop him.

Nikola's teachers couldn't believe it when their young pupil solved impossible problems in his head. He continued his studies at home too. His father hid the candles to prevent Nikola from reading all night. The eager student learned to make his own candles and read on. Nikola wanted to be an inventor, but his father had other ideas. He wanted his son to become a priest like himself.

What Is Engineering?

The word "engineer" comes from the Latin word *ingenium*, meaning cleverness, to create, or invent. Engineers want to know how and why things work. They design and maintain complex products, machines, systems, and structures. There are four kinds of engineers: mechanical, chemical, civil, and electrical engineers.

Nikola Tesla was an electrical engineer. He studied electricity and systems that transmit energy. Now electrical engineers also study electronics and how to make systems that process or transmit information in computers.

Until one night, a doctor was called to the house near the church. As Nikola burned with fever, his desperate father promised him anything if only he got better. The feverish boy whispered one request: He wanted to study engineering.

Nikola's father kept his promise and sent his son to Austria to study engineering. At the university, Nikola saw direct current (DC) electricity created by a Gramme dynamo. But the generator sparked dangerously, and the young student obsessed over a better way to generate electricity. Nikola missed classes and failed in school, eventually returning to his small village. He spent his days there wandering about with his books and a new electrical obsession.

Tesla's Travels

From 1870 to 1884, Nikola moved around going to school or working. Nikola lived in the Austro-Hungarian Empire, which existed in Europe from 1867 to 1918. It was made up of what is now Austria, Italy, and eleven other countries in Eastern Europe.

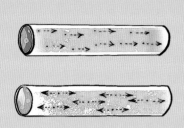

DC vs. AC Electricity

DC, or direct current, and AC, or alternating current, refer to the direction electricity flows through a wire. DC electricity flows in only one direction. Electrons in DC systems lose strength as they travel through wires. That loss of energy can be avoided using AC since its voltage is easier and cheaper to change.

Today, electric companies generate AC. They increase its voltage so it can travel long distances and then decrease its voltage so you can safely use the electricity in your home.

Eventually Nikola found work as a draftsman and an electrician. But he couldn't do his job. He was still obsessed with what he'd seen at the university.

The young dreamer didn't eat or sleep for days as he considered how to solve the DC generator's problems. He thought and thought, until he collapsed and could think no more.

After months in bed, Nikola felt well enough to go out one evening. As he strolled in the setting sun, he was struck by a flash of inspiration. Quickly, he sketched his idea. Nikola had done it! His invention, an alternator, would solve the problems of DC electricity.

Electricity

Electricity can be created when electrons are moved by spinning copper wires inside of a magnetic field. Similar to how a water pump moves water, generators move electrons. Hand cranks, steam, wind, or water can be used to create mechanical energy (movement). This energy causes the wires to spin, which then turns that energy into electric energy.

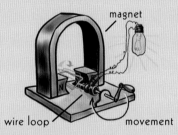

Alternator

An alternator produces electricity this way and gets its name from the alternating current it creates when the wires spin inside the magnetic field. Tesla invented the first alternator that was more efficient than DC electrical generation.

The excited inventor traveled to Paris and Prague to share his discovery. Although he found no interest there, Nikola remembered that in America, Thomas Edison had tried many times before he got an invention right. Perhaps Edison, the inventor of the light bulb and phonograph, would welcome Nikola's improved electrical solution—the alternator.

Nikola took his new invention and set sail for New York City. Battered by storms, the unlucky traveler lost all his possessions and was almost swept overboard before safely arriving.

With only four cents left in his pocket, the eager immigrant found his hero. Edison listened as Nikola described how the alternator would solve problems in Edison's DC electrical systems. Nikola's AC motor would more easily transport electricity over long distances.

Unfortunately, Edison didn't agree to switch to AC. But Edison did recognize the young engineer's genius and hired him.

Nikola immediately started working night and day to help improve Edison's DC dynamos. If he succeeded, Edison promised him $50,000.

Dynamo

A dynamo, or generator, is a machine that takes mechanical energy and turns it into electrical energy using spinning wires and magnetic fields. Dynamos have commutators, which are small parts used to change alternating current to direct current. Edison believed DC current to be safer and better for both lighting and running the electric motors of that time.

Energy in the form of direct current can be stored in a battery. It is still used in many devices today, such as flashlights.

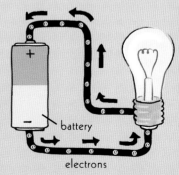

battery

electrons

After working six long months, Nikola reported his improvements to Edison and requested his payment. Edison laughed. The American inventor had never planned on giving Nikola that money no matter how hard he worked.

Nikola quit in disgust.

But soon two businessmen saw promise in the unemployed inventor. With their money, Nikola developed an improved arc lighting company called Tesla Electric Light and Manufacturing. But when Nikola again wanted to use electricity generated from his alternator, they fired the inventor from the company he built.

Early Electric Lights

The arc lamp was the first successful form of electric lamp used to light public streets. In 1844, these lamps produced a very bright light created by an electrical current running between two carbon rods. Arc lights were less expensive than early lamps that used whale oil or animal fat. Edison had invented the first commercially successful incandescent light bulb in 1879. Incandescent light bulbs use a thin wire heated to such a high temperature that they glow.

Now, to survive, Nikola took jobs digging ditches for Edison's electric cables, which snaked over and under the streets of New York. This wasn't Nikola's American dream, but he didn't stop talking about his invention and ideas.

George Westinghouse was an American inventor who, like Nikola, also believed in AC electricity. When Westinghouse heard Nikola's bright ideas, he hired him immediately. Westinghouse paid Nikola well for his patents.

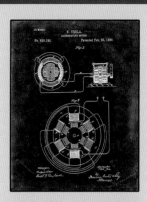

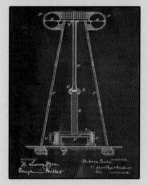

Patent

A patent says that only an inventor can make or sell their invention. A royalty is the money made from letting others use or sell the new invention.

Over his lifetime, Nikola had 278 patents awarded to him from 26 countries.

In 1893, for the first time, the World's Fair was to be powered by electricity. When darkness fell on opening night, buildings and fountains sparkled with light. Twenty-seven million visitors marveled at seeing such brilliance.

Nikola and Westinghouse were chosen to illuminate the Chicago World's Fair since their AC cost much less than Edison's DC. Westinghouse Electric Company workers installed 100,000 lights powered by 12 brand-new thousand-horsepower generators and amazed the world. Nikola Tesla finally proved that AC electricity was the way to go.

Westinghouse Electric Company then built one of the world's first AC hydroelectric power plants, completed in 1895. The plant used water from Niagara Falls to turn Nikola's AC generators. Nikola's dream of harnessing the power of waterfalls had finally come true.

How Water Creates Electricity

Hydroelectricity is created by generators that are powered by moving water. The water flows down pipes, which lead to a turbine. The pressure from the moving water spins rotors on the turbine. The turbine is connected to a generator that creates electricity when the turbine spins. Then the electricity is sent to homes through copper cables.

The young dreamer didn't rest. Even though Nikola faced rejection and hardship, he didn't stop. He was brave and proved to be a different kind of thinker.

Over the years, Nikola went on to invent the fluorescent light, parts that made wireless radio, remote-controlled vehicles, X-rays, concepts for guided missiles and their defense shields, robots, and radar. He even created the motor that is used today in a fast, electric sports car. This car is named after the unlikely inventor with brilliant visions, Nikola Tesla.

GLOSSARY

alternating current (AWL-tuhr-nayt-ing KUR-uhnt)—electrical current that switches direction many times a second

alternator (AWL-tuhr-nay-ter)—a device that produces alternating current

arc lamp (AHRK LAMP)—a lamp that uses an arc of electric current between two electrodes to produce light

atom (AT-uhm)—the smallest particle of an element that has all the properties of that element

direct current (duh-REKT KUR-uhnt)—current that always moves in the same direction

dynamo (DYE-nuh-moh)—a machine for converting the power of a turning wheel into electricity; a generator

electricity (i-lek-TRISS-uh-tee)—a form of energy caused by the motion of protons and electrons

engineer (en-juh-NEER)—a person who is specially trained to plan, design, or build machines and large structures

generator (JEN-uh-ray-tur)—a machine that produces energy by turning a magnet inside a coil of wire

hydroelectricity (hye-droh-i-lek-TRISS-uh-tee)—a form of energy caused by flowing water

incandescent (in-kuhn-DES-uhnt)—producing light as a consequence of being heated to a high temperature

mechanical energy (muh-KAN-i-kuhl EN-ur-jee)—the energy that an object has because of its position and motion

patent (PAT-uhnt)—a legal document giving someone sole rights to make or sell a product

phonograph (FOH-nuh-graf)—a machine that reproduces sounds that have been recorded in the grooves of a record

rotor (ROH-tur)—the part of an electrical machine that turns

royalty (ROI-uhl-tee)—a payment made to the owner of a patent or copyright for the use of it

static electricity (STAT-ik i-lek-TRISS-uh-tee)—the buildup of an electrical charge on the surface of an object

turbine (TUR-bine)—a machine with blades that can be turned by wind or a moving fluid such as steam or water

voltage (VOHL-tij)—the force of an electrical current

AFTERWORD

Although Tesla succeeded in having his bright dreams come true, his story didn't necessarily have a happy ending. Thinking more about invention than how to successfully run a business, Tesla lost money and control of his patents to investors. Later, Edison battled Westinghouse and Tesla for electrical dominance. Unconcerned with money, Tesla gave up significant royalties to keep Westinghouse's company afloat.

Tesla had troubles socially too. If living today, he would probably be diagnosed with autism spectrum disorder. Like many on the autism spectrum, Nikola would focus on his interests to the exclusion of most everything else. This intense focus and his ability to visualize and solve complex problems in his head may have contributed to his success in science and engineering.

Unfortunately, Tesla had so many obsessions and phobias that many thought him unbalanced. He was terrified of hair, jewelry, and germs, and he had an intense sensitivity to light and sound. He was obsessed with pigeons and the number 3. He fed thousands of pigeons over the years, often bringing ailing ones home to his rented room. Tesla said, "But there was one pigeon, a beautiful bird. . . . I had only to wish and call her and she would come flying to me. I loved that pigeon. . . . As long as I had her, there was a purpose in my life."

His strange habits led others to dismiss Tesla as insane. When the inventor tried to promote his newest laser technology, which he believed would prevent future wars, people dismissed him. With time, forgotten and ignored, Tesla retreated to his pigeons and lived alone and in poverty until he died at age 86.

"Money does not represent such a value that men have placed upon it. All my money has been invested into experiments with which I have made new discoveries enabling mankind to have a little easier life."

—Nikola Tesla

ABOUT THE AUTHOR-ILLUSTRATOR

After spending her grade school years doodling in science class, most often taught by tired coaches, Tracy Dockray migrated with her chihuahua and vintage motorcycles from West Texas to New York City to study art. She eventually expanded her canine companionship to a family and traded in her two wheels for a minivan. This mind-blowing experience has given Tracy new insights into children's books and their audience. She is ecstatic to have illustrated more than 25 books, including an edition of Beverly Cleary's Ramona series, The Mouse and the Motorcycle series, and most recently, Nicole C. Kear's The Fix-It Friends series. *Bright Dreams* is her attempt to bring to light Nikola Tesla's story and explain electricity, a fascinating subject that she obviously missed while she was doodling. Although Tracy studied fine art in school, she has come to the happy conclusion that drawing pictures for children's books is the finest art she knows.

TESLA TIMELINE

1856 - Nikola Tesla is born in modern-day Croatia.

1863 - Tesla's older brother dies in horseback riding accident.

1870 - Becomes passionate about math and physics.

1873 - Bedridden for nine months with cholera.

1875 - Attends college, becomes obsessed with electricity, and drops out.

1878 - Finds first job as a draftsman for an engineering firm.

1881 - Works as an electrician at the Budapest Telephone Exchange.

1882 - Obsesses over solving the riddle of AC electricity and collapses.

1884 - Sails to New York City to meet Thomas Edison.

1885 - Quits working on Edison's DC machinery after a pay dispute.

1886 - Creates Tesla Electric Light and Manufacturing but loses investment.

1887 - Works as ditchdigger for two dollars a day.

1888 - Gives lecture on AC motors to electrical engineers at Columbia University.

1889 - Tesla's AC versus Edison's DC, which came to be known as the War of the Currents, is at its peak.

1891 - Patents the Tesla Coil that produces high-voltage AC electricity.

1893 - With the help of Westinghouse, Tesla electrifies the Chicago World's Fair.

1894 - One year before Wilhelm Röntgen, Tesla creates X-rays with a vacuum tube he'd invented. He called the pictures shadowgraphs.

1895 - Sends his X-rays to Röntgen to show him he'd developed X-rays as well.

1898 - Demonstrates remote-controlled boat.

1901 - Builds Wardenclyffe Tower in hopes of wirelessly transmitting electricity, sounds, and images.

1915 - Protests Marconi's radio patent, since Tesla had accomplished this first.

1916 - Tesla declares bankruptcy.

1917 - Wardenclyffe Tower is torn down for scrap to pay Tesla's debts.

1922 - Tesla is heartbroken after beloved pet pigeon dies.

1924 - Develops new car engine for the Budd Company.

1930 - Tesla is asked to leave his hotel residence after complaints of pigeon droppings and unpaid bills.

1931 - Tesla turns 75 and receives many congratulatory letters including one from Albert Einstein.

1935 - Writes paper about a particle machine he could invent that would end war.

1937 - Tesla is hit by a car and never completely recovers.

1938 - Receives Immigrant Welfare Honor in recognition of his contributions to American life.

1943 - Tesla dies alone in his New York City hotel room at age 86.

SELECT BIBLIOGRAPHY

American Experience: Tesla, season 29, episode 7, written and produced by David Grubin; executive producer, Mark Samels, aired October 18, 2016, on PBS, (Boston, MA: WGBH Educational Foundation, 2016), https://www.pbs.org/wgbh/americanexperience/films/tesla/

Carlson, W. Bernard. *Tesla: Inventor of the Electrical Age.* Princeton, NJ: Princeton University Press, 2013.

"Nikola Tesla Universe." Tesla Universe. Accessed October 28, 2019. https://teslauniverse.com

Nye, Bill. "Electricity." Accessed October 28, 2019. https://billnye.com/the-science-guy/electricity

O'Neill, John J. *Prodigal Genius; The Life of Nikola Tesla.* New York: I. Washburn, Inc., 1944.

Seifer, Marc J. *Wizard: The Life and Times of Nikola Tesla: Biography of a Genius.* Secaucus, NJ: Carol Pub., 1996.

Tesla: Master of Lightning, directed, written, and produced by Robert Uth; executive producer, Phylis Geller (Washington, DC: New Voyage Communications, Inc., 2000), VHS.

Tesla, Nikola. *My Inventions: the Autobiography of Nikola Tesla / edited, with an introduction, by Ben Johnston.* Williston, VT: Hart Bros., 1982.

SOURCE NOTES

"Let the future tell the truth . . ." Dragislav L. Petkovic, "A Visit to Nikola Tesla," *Politika*, April 27, 1927.

"Money does not represent . . ." Ibid.

"But there was one pigeon . . ." John J. O'Neill. *Prodigal Genius: The Life of Nikola Tesla.* New York: I. Washburn, Inc., 1944. p. 316.

READ MORE

Cimarusti, Nick. *Thomas Edison: Lighting a Revolution.* Huntington Beach, CA: Teacher Created Materials, Inc., 2019.

Gigliotti, Jim. *Who Was Nikola Tesla?* New York: Penguin Workshop, an imprint of Penguin Random House, 2018.

Sobey, Ed. *Electrical Engineering: Learn It, Try It!* North Mankato, MN: Capstone Press, a Capstone imprint, 2018.

INTERNET SITES

Build an Electric Highway
https://pbskids.org/designsquad/parentseducators/resources/electric_highway.html

More about Nikola Tesla
https://www.youtube.com/watch?v=g1DqaqBiVRY

Where Does Electricity Come From?
https://www.nationalgeographic.org/media/where-does-electricity-come/

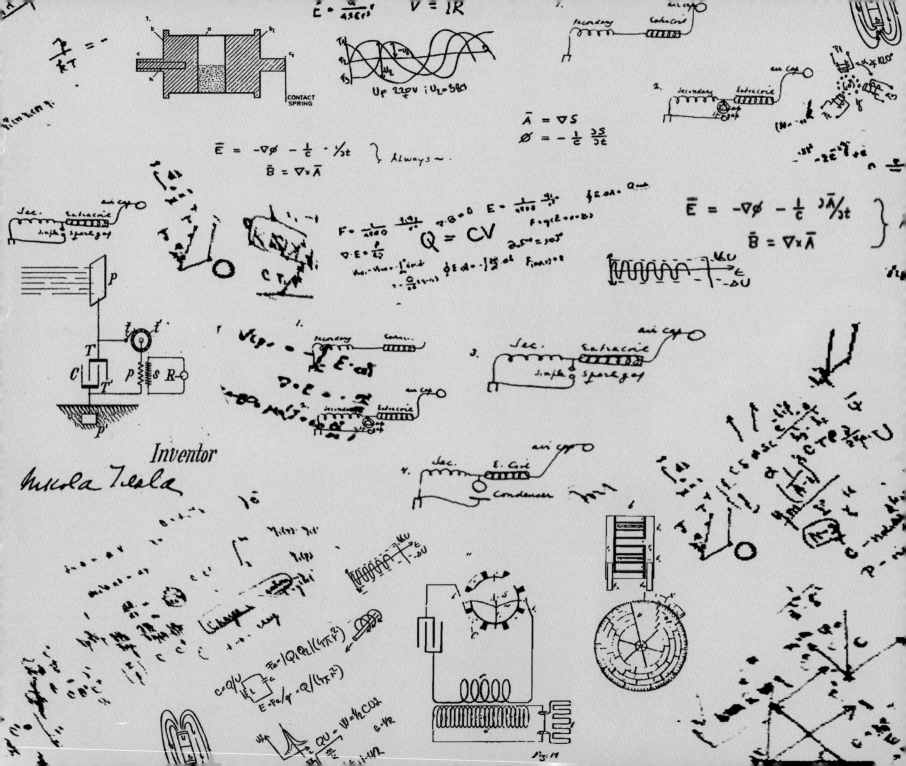

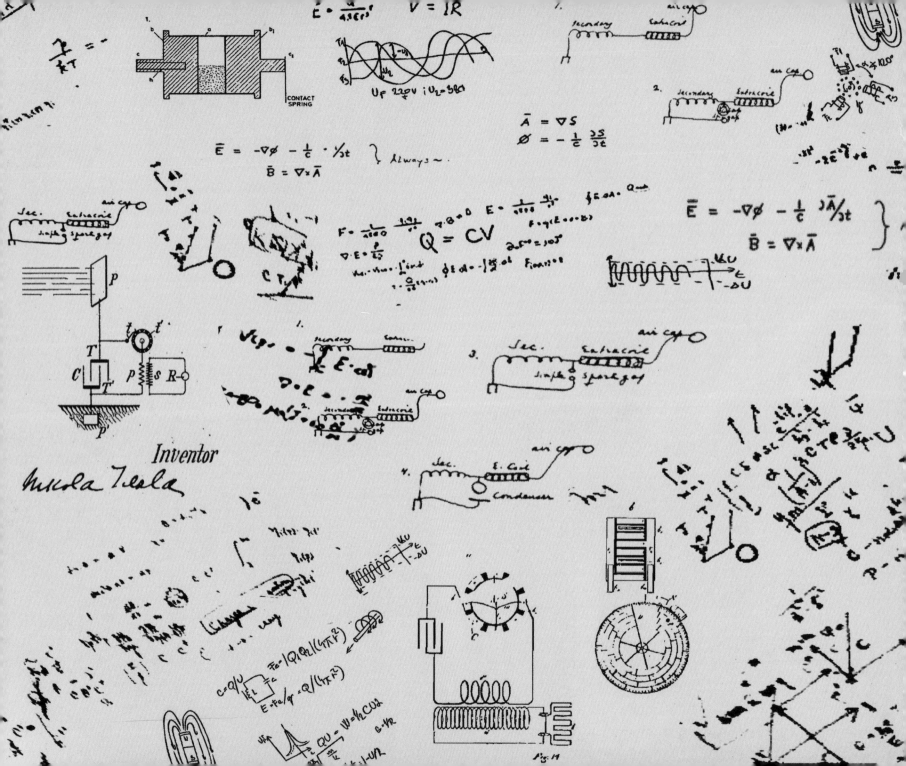